Little Burro

with scripture describing an humble servant

Third in the GOD MADE ALL THINGS series

By Marion W. Richardson

Copyright 2015
Marion W. Richardson

All rights reserved.
No part of this book may be used or reproduced without written permission except for brief quotations for review purposes.

Marion W. Richardson
3660 Highway 41
Stanley, New Mexico 87056-9708
www.marionwrichardson.com

ISBN-13: 978-1512096019
ISBN-10: 1512096016
First Edition

All scripture references are to the
King James Version of the Holy Bible.

Forward

The Bible records favorable comments regarding the faithful servant. Jesus states in Matthew 25:21 that he will make the servant "ruler over many things" because he was "faithful over a few things." In the Psalms, we are urged to "Make a joyful noise unto the LORD, all ye lands. Serve the LORD with gladness." (Psalm 100:1-2)

The humble little donkey, or burro, has been used as an example of a faithful servant. Jacob, Abraham's grandson, uses the donkey to describe Issachar, one of his sons, when he says, "Issachar is a strong ass couching down between two burdens: And he saw that rest was good, and the land that it was pleasant; and bowed his shoulder to bear, and became a servant unto tribute." (Genesis 49:14-15) The burro was used to carry cargo throughout the promised land of Israel. In 1 Chronicles 12:40 tribes joined King David as they "brought bread on asses, and on camels, and on mules, and on oxen, and meat, meal, cakes of figs, and bunches of raisins, and wine, and oil, and oxen, and sheep abundantly: for there was joy in Israel."

Perhaps the most endearing story of the burro in the Bible is that of the young "colt" of a donkey which awaits his master Jesus' command that he be loosed from where he is tied and brought to Jesus who, in his own words, "hath need of him." This was the occasion for which Little Burro had been prepared, carrying his master triumphantly into Jerusalem.

In Little Burro, I have identified qualities of the burro that relate to the Christian who wishes to serve the Lord. It is my prayer that you will learn the ways of a servant as you follow Little Burro on his path.

Love,

Miss Marion

Marion

Little Burro is a faithful servant.
God made him that way.
For He will use him some day.

Little Burro finds the good path.

God made him that way.
For He will use him some day.

Little Burro sounds his alarm.

God made him that way.
For He will use him some day.

Little Burro listens
for his master.

God made him that way.
For He will use him some day.

Little Burro stands firm.

God made him that way.
For He will use him some day.

Little Burro remembers.

God made him that way.
For He will use him some day.

Little Burro surveys the land.

God made him that way.
For He will use him some day.

Little Burro takes time to rest.

God made him that way.
For He will use him some day.

Little Burro makes sure he is fed.

God made him that way.
For He will use him some day.

Little Burro will do what is safe.

God made him that way.
For He will use him some day.

Little Burro will be steady and strong.

God made him that way.
For He will use him some day.

Little Burro will guard his herd.

God made him that way.
For He will use him some day.

Little Burro will carry his master.

Hallelujah, we say.
For God used him this day.

You too were made in a way

that God will use you some day!

KEY SCRIPTURE VERSE

Proverbs 2:1-9
1 My son, if thou wilt receive my words, and hide my commandments with thee; 2 So that thou incline thine ear unto wisdom, and apply thine heart to understanding; 3 Yea, if thou criest after knowledge, and liftest up thy voice for understanding; 4 If thou seekest her as silver, and searchest for her as for hid treasures; 5 Then shalt thou understand the fear of the LORD, and find the knowledge of God. 6 For the LORD giveth wisdom: out of his mouth cometh knowledge and understanding. 7 He layeth up sound wisdom for the righteous: he is a buckler to them that walk uprightly. 8 He keepeth the paths of judgment, and preserveth the way of his saints.
9 Then shalt thou understand righteousness, and judgment, and equity; yea, every good path.

1 Peter 5:6
6 Humble yourselves therefore under the mighty hand of God, that he may exalt you in due time:

Psalm 100:2-3
2 Serve the LORD with gladness: come before his presence with singing. 3 Know ye that the LORD he is God: it is he that hath made us, and not we ourselves; we are his people, and the sheep of his pasture.

LITTLE BURRO IS A FAITHFUL SERVANT

Matthew 25:20-22
20 And so he that had received five talents came and brought other five talents, saying, Lord, thou deliveredst unto me five talents: behold, I have gained beside them five talents more. 21   His lord said unto him, Well done, thou good and faithful servant: thou hast been faithful over a few things, I will make thee ruler over many things: enter thou into the joy of thy lord. 22   He also that had received two talents came and said, Lord, thou deliveredst unto me two talents: behold, I have gained two other talents beside them.

Revelation 17:14B
14B and the Lamb shall overcome them: for he is Lord of lords, and King of kings: and they that are with him are called, and chosen, and faithful.

Psalm 2:10-11
10 Be wise now therefore, O ye kings: be instructed, ye judges of the earth. 11 Serve the LORD with fear, and rejoice with trembling.

Galatians 5:13
13 For, brethren, ye have been called unto liberty; only use not liberty for an occasion to the flesh, but by love serve one another.

Colossians 3:23-24

23 And whatsoever ye do, do it heartily, as to the Lord, and not unto men; 24 Knowing that of the Lord ye shall receive the reward of the inheritance: for ye serve the Lord Christ.

LITTLE BURRO WILL FIND THE GOOD PATH

Psalm 16:11

11 Thou wilt shew me the path of life: in thy presence is fulness of joy; at thy right hand there are pleasures for evermore.

Proverbs 4:18

18 But the path of the just is as the shining light, that shineth more and more unto the perfect day.

Proverbs 4:26-27

26 Ponder the path of thy feet, and let all thy ways be established. 27 Turn not to the right hand nor to the left: remove thy foot from evil.

Proverbs 16:9

9 A man's heart deviseth his way: but the LORD directeth his steps.

Proverbs 3:5-6

5 Trust in the LORD with all thine heart; and lean not unto thine own understanding. 6 In all thy ways acknowledge him, and he shall direct thy paths.

Matthew 7:13-14

13 Enter ye in at the strait gate: for wide is the gate, and broad is the way, that leadeth to destruction, and many there be which go in thereat: 14 Because strait is the gate, and narrow is the way, which leadeth unto life, and few there be that find it.

Psalm 25:8-10

8 Good and upright is the LORD: therefore will he teach sinners in the way. 9 The meek will he guide in judgment: and the meek will he teach his way. 10 All the paths of the LORD are mercy and truth unto such as keep his covenant and his testimonies.

Galatians 6:4-7

4 But let every man prove his own work, and then shall he have rejoicing in himself alone, and not in another. 5 For every man shall bear his own burden. 6 Let him that is taught in the word communicate unto him that teacheth in all good things. 7 Be not deceived; God is not mocked: for whatsoever a man soweth, that shall he also reap.

Ephesians 6:6-8

6 Not with eyeservice, as menpleasers; but as the servants of Christ, doing the will of God from the heart; 7 With good will doing service, as to the Lord, and not to men: 8 Knowing that whatsoever good thing any man doeth, the same shall he receive of the Lord, whether he be bond or free.

LITTLE BURRO SOUNDS HIS ALARM

Psalm 142:1-6
1 I cried unto the LORD with my voice; with my voice unto the LORD did I make my supplication. 2 I poured out my complaint before him; I shewed before him my trouble. 3 When my spirit was overwhelmed within me, then thou knewest my path. In the way wherein I walked have they privily laid a snare for me.
4 I looked on my right hand, and beheld, but there was no man that would know me: refuge failed me; no man cared for my soul.
5 I cried unto thee, O LORD: I said, Thou art my refuge and my portion in the land of the living. 6 Attend unto my cry; for I am brought very low: deliver me from my persecutors; for they are stronger than I.

Psalm 78:1-3
1 Give ear, O my people, to my law: incline your ears to the words of my mouth. 2 I will open my mouth in a parable: I will utter dark sayings of old: 3 Which we have heard and known, and our fathers have told us.

LITTLE BURRO LISTENS FOR HIS MASTER

Exodus 15:26
26 And said, If thou wilt diligently hearken to the voice of the LORD thy God, and wilt do that which is right in his sight, and wilt give ear to his commandments, and keep all his statutes, I will put none of these diseases upon thee, which I have brought upon the Egyptians: for I am the LORD that healeth thee.

Deuteronomy 28:1-2

1 And it shall come to pass, if thou shalt hearken diligently unto the voice of the LORD thy God, to observe and to do all his commandments which I command thee this day, that the LORD thy God will set thee on high above all nations of the earth: 2 And all these blessings shall come on thee, and overtake thee, if thou shalt hearken unto the voice of the LORD thy God.

Deuteronomy 30:10

10 If thou shalt hearken unto the voice of the LORD thy God, to keep his commandments and his statutes which are written in this book of the law, and if thou turn unto the LORD thy God with all thine heart, and with all thy soul.

Proverbs 4:20-23

20 My son, attend to my words; incline thine ear unto my sayings. 21 Let them not depart from thine eyes; keep them in the midst of thine heart. 22 For they are life unto those that find them, and health to all their flesh. 23 Keep thy heart with all diligence; for out of it are the issues of life.

Matthew 13:9

9 Who hath ears to hear, let him hear.

LITTLE BURRO STANDS FIRM

Psalm 37:23-24

23 The steps of a good man are ordered by the LORD: and he delighteth in his way. 24 Though he fall, he shall not be utterly cast down: for the LORD upholdeth him with his hand.

LITTLE BURRO REMEMBERS

Numbers 15:37-41
37 And the LORD spake unto Moses, saying, 38 Speak unto the children of Israel, and bid them that they make them fringes in the borders of their garments throughout their generations, and that they put upon the fringe of the borders a ribband of blue:
39 And it shall be unto you for a fringe, that ye may look upon it, and remember all the commandments of the LORD, and do them; and that ye seek not after your own heart and your own eyes, after which ye use to go a whoring: 40 That ye may remember, and do all my commandments, and be holy unto your God.
41 I am the LORD your God, which brought you out of the land of Egypt, to be your God: I am the LORD your God.

Deuteronomy 8:18
18 But thou shalt remember the LORD thy God: for it is he that giveth thee power to get wealth, that he may establish his covenant which he sware unto thy fathers, as it is this day.

1 Chronicles 16:11-12
11 Seek the LORD and his strength, seek his face continually.
12 Remember his marvellous works that he hath done, his wonders, and the judgments of his mouth;

Ecclesiastes 12:1
1 Remember now thy Creator in the days of thy youth, while the evil days come not, nor the years draw nigh, when thou shalt say, I have no pleasure in them;

Isaiah 46:9

9 Remember the former things of old: for I am God, and there is none else; I am God, and there is none like me,

LITTLE BURRO SURVEYS THE LAND

Numbers 13:1-2

1 And the LORD spake unto Moses, saying, 2 Send thou men, that they may search the land of Canaan, which I give unto the children of Israel: of every tribe of their fathers shall ye send a man, every one a ruler among them.

Joshua 18:4

4 Give out from among you three men for each tribe: and I will send them, and they shall rise, and go through the land, and describe it according to the inheritance of them; and they shall come again to me.

Judges 18:2a

2 And the children of Dan sent of their family five men from their coasts, men of valour, from Zorah, and from Eshtaol, to spy out the land, and to search it; and they said unto them, Go, search the land:

Lamentations 3:40-41

40 Let us search and try our ways, and turn again to the LORD.
41 Let us lift up our heart with our hands unto God in the heavens.

LITLE BURRO TAKES TIME TO REST

Leviticus 23:3
3 Six days shall work be done: but the seventh day is the sabbath of rest, an holy convocation; ye shall do no work therein: it is the sabbath of the LORD in all your dwellings.

Psalm 37:7a
7 Rest in the LORD, and wait patiently for him:

LITTLE BURRO MAKES SURE HE IS FED

Genesis 2:9a
9 And out of the ground made the LORD God to grow every tree that is pleasant to the sight, and good for food; the tree of life also in the midst of the garden,

1 Chronicles 12:40
40 Moreover they that were nigh them, even unto Issachar and Zebulun and Naphtali, brought bread on asses, and on camels, and on mules, and on oxen, and meat, meal, cakes of figs, and bunches of raisins, and wine, and oil, and oxen, and sheep abundantly: for there was joy in Israel.

Genesis 1:29-31

29 And God said, Behold, I have given you every herb bearing seed, which is upon the face of all the earth, and every tree, in the which is the fruit of a tree yielding seed; to you it shall be for meat. 30 And to every beast of the earth, and to every fowl of the air, and to every thing that creepeth upon the earth, wherein there is life, I have given every green herb for meat: and it was so. 31 And God saw every thing that he had made, and, behold, it was very good. And the evening and the morning were the sixth day.

Ezekiel 34:27

27 And the tree of the field shall yield her fruit, and the earth shall yield her increase, and they shall be safe in their land, and shall know that I am the LORD, when I have broken the bands of their yoke, and delivered them out of the hand of those that served themselves of them.

Acts 14:17b

17 in that he did good, and gave us rain from heaven, and fruitful seasons, filling our hearts with food and gladness.

LITTLE BURRO WILL DO WHAT IS SAFE

Jeremiah 6:16a

16 Thus saith the LORD, Stand ye in the ways, and see, and ask for the old paths, where is the good way, and walk therein, and ye shall find rest for your souls.

LITTLE BURRO WILL BE STEADY AND STRONG

Deuteronomy 31:6

6 Be strong and of a good courage, fear not, nor be afraid of them: for the LORD thy God, he it is that doth go with thee; he will not fail thee, nor forsake thee.

1 Chronicles 28:10

10 Take heed now; for the LORD hath chosen thee to build an house for the sanctuary: be strong, and do it.

Daniel 10:19

19 And said, O man greatly beloved, fear not: peace be unto thee, be strong, yea, be strong. And when he had spoken unto me, I was strengthened, and said, Let my lord speak; for thou hast strengthened me.

1 Corinthians 16:13

13 Watch ye, stand fast in the faith, quit you like men, be strong.

LITTLE BURRO WILL GUARD HIS HERD

Psalm 138:6-7

6 Though the LORD be high, yet hath he respect unto the lowly: but the proud he knoweth afar off. 7 Though I walk in the midst of trouble, thou wilt revive me: thou shalt stretch forth thine hand against the wrath of mine enemies, and thy right hand shall save me.

LITTLE BURRO WILL CARRY HIS MASTER

Zechariah 9:9

9 Rejoice greatly, O daughter of Zion; shout, O daughter of Jerusalem: behold, thy King cometh unto thee: he is just, and having salvation; lowly, and riding upon an ass, and upon a colt the foal of an ass.

Colossians 3:22-24

22 Servants, obey in all things your masters according to the flesh; not with eyeservice, as menpleasers; but in singleness of heart, fearing God: 23 And whatsoever ye do, do it heartily, as to the Lord, and not unto men; 24 Knowing that of the Lord ye shall receive the reward of the inheritance: for ye serve the Lord Christ.

1 Peter 2:18-21

18 Servants, be subject to your masters with all fear; not only to the good and gentle, but also to the froward. 19 For this is thankworthy, if a man for conscience toward God endure grief, suffering wrongfully. 20 For what glory is it, if, when ye be buffeted for your faults, ye shall take it patiently? but if, when ye do well, and suffer for it, ye take it patiently, this is acceptable with God. 21 For even hereunto were ye called: because Christ also suffered for us, leaving us an example, that ye should follow his steps:

Titus 2:9-10

9 Exhort servants to be obedient unto their own masters, and to please them well in all things; not answering again; 10 Not purloining, but shewing all good fidelity; that they may adorn the doctrine of God our Saviour in all things.

YOU, TOO, WERE MADE IN A WAY THAT GOD WILL USE YOU ONE DAY

Psalm 31:1-3 (KJV)
1 In thee, O LORD, do I put my trust; let me never be ashamed: deliver me in thy righteousness. 2 Bow down thine ear to me; deliver me speedily: be thou my strong rock, for an house of defence to save me. 3 For thou art my rock and my fortress; therefore for thy name's sake lead me, and guide me.

Psalm 32:7-8
7 Thou art my hiding place; thou shalt preserve me from trouble; thou shalt compass me about with songs of deliverance. Selah. 8 I will instruct thee and teach thee in the way which thou shalt go: I will guide thee with mine eye.

Hebrews 6:12-15
12 That ye be not slothful, but followers of them who through faith and patience inherit the promises. 13 For when God made promise to Abraham, because he could swear by no greater, he sware by himself, 14 Saying, Surely blessing I will bless thee, and multiplying I will multiply thee. 15 And so, after he had patiently endured, he obtained the promise.

Matthew 11:29-30
29 Take my yoke upon you, and learn of me; for I am meek and lowly in heart: and ye shall find rest unto your souls. 30 For my yoke is easy, and my burden is light.

Hebrews 12:2-3
2 Looking unto Jesus the author and finisher of our faith; who for the joy that was set before him endured the cross, despising the shame, and is set down at the right hand of the throne of God.
3 For consider him that endured such contradiction of sinners against himself, lest ye be wearied and faint in your minds.

Arabian Leopard	 Arabian Oryx	 Arabian Single Hump Camel	 Caspian Turtle
 Caracal Desert Lynx	 Jerusalem Donkey	 Ringed Turtle Dove	 European Bee-eater
 European Green Toad	 Fire Salamander	 Hedgehog	 Hoopoe Bird

These are animals from Israel

Nubian Ibex	Jerboa mouse	Lamb	Marbled Polecat
Mediterranean Spur-thighed Tortoise	Middle East Tree Frog	Mountain Gazelle	Purple Swamphen
Red Fox	Rose-ringed Parakeet	Sand Cat	Yellow Hammer

where Little Burro lives.

Further Explanation:

1. It is paramount that Christians understand that we are to find joy in the role of servant. In Matthew 25:21-22 Jesus says, "Well done, thou good and faithful servant: thou has been faithful over a few things, I will make thee ruler over many things: enter thou into the joy of the Lord." Being a faithful servant is a very good thing. God expects that we will want to serve Him with joy. Galatians 5:13b says "by love serve one another." Colossians goes on to say, "And whatsoever ye do, do it heartily, as to the Lord...for ye serve the Lord Christ." (Colossians 3:23-24)

2. Notice that Little Burro does not stumble upon a path. He does not wake up in the morning and choose the easiest path. No, he finds the *good* path. This means he seeks it out and makes the conscious choice to walk on that path. There are so many wonderful verses in the Bible regarding the "path." Ask and God will show you the wise path, the one He has chosen for you to follow.

3. When Little Burro sounds his alarm, or brays, his fellow creatures listen. God will place it on His servant's heart to warn others. He fills us with His Spirit who will in turn warn us when danger is in our midst. Psalm 142:5b reads, "Thou art my refuge and my portion in the land of the living." Be alert to all warning signs.

4. Not only does Little Burro listen *to* the commands of His master and obeys them, he also listens *for* the voice of His master. God says to "incline your ears to the words of my mouth." (Psalm 78:1b) May this encourage you to read God's word and listen for Him to speak to you through His words, through His still voice as you pray, and through the wisdom of those fellow Christians He puts in your path.

5. Little Burro is not one to sway in the wind. He is firm in his love *of* and committment *to* the Lord. Ephesians 6:13 says "Wherefore take unto you the whole armour of God, that ye may be able to withstand in the evil day, and having done all, to stand." God is not looking for lukewarm servants. He wants those who will "Be strong and of a good courage, fear not, nor be afraid..." (Deuteronomy 31:6)

6. It is important to be able to recall the wonderful things that God has done, not just for you individually, but His works throughout time. At one time, God even told Moses to weave a blue thread into the garments to remind the people of God's commandments. It is a beneficial practice for Christians to remember. Memorize scripture. Learn from your Bible. Study and practice. Learn more and more each day.

7. As Little Burro surveys the land, he is studying, searching, and and making observations. We too should be aware of things that are happening around us. Perhaps God will put a person who is hurting and in need of comfort in your path. Be alert to the world around you. God sends signs and wonders for us to observe. It is also important for us to search our own hearts, souls, and lives. Ask God to show you things about yourself. Allow Him to search you and reveal things to you.

8. God has taught us to rest. The Israelites were commanded to rest on the Sabbath. Now we rest in Jesus and the salvation He has won us. In addition, rest in the peace that He gives us. The path of Jesus is that "good way" that brings rest to our tired souls. (Jeremiah 6:16)

9. Little Burro knows the importance of being fed. He makes sure he gets his needed nourishment so that he can be ready for service. God has given us good foods for our body. We should care for our body as it is the temple of the Lord. (1 Corinthians 6:19) We should also be fed with God's word and produce good fruit as referenced in the fruit of the spirit found in Galatians 5:22.

10. Little Burro is careful not to get himself into situations that might be dangerous. Many of the characteristics of Little Burro are to protect him. Like Little Burro, we need to do as advised in 1 Peter 5:8, "Be sober, be vigilant; because your adversary the devil, as a roaring lion, walketh about, seeking whom he may devour:" Little Burro understands about those lions, leopards, lynx and foxes too.

11. Donkeys are known for their ability to endure. The servant needs to have lasting energy and patience. Sometimes, enduring means suffering. The weight that Little Burro has to carry might become a burden. God encourages his servants to not grow weary or faint. Jesus says, "Take my yoke upon you, and learn of me... for my yoke is easy, and my burden is light." (Matthew 11:29) When we get tired, it is Jesus who strengthens and refreshes us.

12. Little Burro watches out for his fellow animals. When rebuilding the walls of Jerusalem, Nehemiah made sure that the workers were guarded. (Nehemiah 4:22) Many "guards" are mentioned throughout the Bible. One special one was Benaiah, the son of Jehoiada. He is mentioned in 2 Samuel 23:23 and is described as being "more honorable" than thirty of King David's guard, being set over the entire group. Watch over your hearts as well. As Philippians 4:7 (KJV) states "And the peace of God, which passeth all understanding, shall keep your hearts and minds through Christ Jesus." Other versions of the Bible use the word "guard" in place of "keep."

13. God prepares each of us for a time in which He will use us. Little Burro's physical and behavioral traits were important for his use as a servant. Just like Esther who was told by her cousin, Mordecai, in Esther 4:14, "who knoweth whether thou art come to the kingdom for such a time as this?" God's plan for Little Burro was so defined that it was prophesied in Zechariah 9:9, "Rejoice greatly, O daughter of Zion; shout, O daughter of Jerusalem: behold, thy King cometh unto thee: he is just, and having salvation; lowly, and riding upon an ass, and upon a colt the foal of an ass." As told in the New Testament Book of Luke, Jesus said, "Go ye into the village over against you; in the which at your entering ye shall find a colt tied, whereon yet never man sat: loose him, and bring him hither." (Luke 19:30) Until that day, Little Burro had not carried a man. This truly was the most important mission of his young life, to carry the King of kings. The people shouted, "Blessed be the King that cometh in the name of the Lord: peace in heaven, and glory in the highest." (Luke 19:38) Servants carry out the will of their master. Christians carry the message of The Gospel as commanded by Jesus in Matthew 28:19-20. "Go ye therefore, and teach all nations, baptizing them in the name of the Father, and of the Son, and of the Holy Ghost: Teaching them to observe all things whatsoever I have commanded you: and, lo, I am with you alway, even unto the end of the world."

14. God knows everything about us. He created us in his own image. (Genesis 1:26) Psalm 139:2-4 says, "Thou knowest my downsitting and mine uprising, thou understandest my thought afar off. Thou compassest my path and my lying down, and art acquainted with all my ways. For there is not a word in my tongue, but, lo, O LORD, thou knowest it altogether." Our skills, our talents, our unique personalities, our likes and dislikes, all of these things are part of God's design. They work together, as Romans 8:28 assures us, "we know that all things work together for good to them that love God, to them who are the called according to his purpose."

15. May I encourage each and every reader, young and old, to learn from Little Burro. Allow God to form you into a usable servant. As He says, "I ... will refine them as silver is refined, and will try them as gold is tried: they shall call on my name, and I will hear them: I will say, It is my people: and they shall say, The LORD is my God." (Zechariah 13:9) You were made in such a way that He indeed will use you some day.

Notes and Thoughts

Notes and Thoughts

Bibliography

Dake, Finis J. The KJV Dake Annotated Reference Bible. Lawrenceville, Georgia: Dake Bible Publishers, 1963.

Holy Bible: King James Version WORDsearch CROSS e-book.

http://www.Bibledonkeys.com/id=131 (May 2015).

http://www.fromthegrapevine.com/nature/israels-10-beautiful-animals (May 2015).

http://www.fromthegrapevine.com/nature/israels-10-beautiful-birds (May 2015).

http://www.jta.org/2012/04/23/news-opinion/the-telegraph/10-photos-of-animals-common-to-israel-doing-awesome-things (May 2015).

http://www.mikesdonkeys.co.uk/facts.html (May 2015).

http://www.natureisrael.com/creatures.html#turtle (May 2015).

Made in the USA
Charleston, SC
08 July 2015